BUTTERFLIES

Sally Morgan

W

FRANKLIN WATTS

LONDON•SYDNEY

© 2005 Franklin Watts
First published in 2005
by Franklin Watts
96 Leonard Street
London EC2A 4XD

Franklin Watts Australia
45-51 Huntley Street
Alexandria NSW 2015

Produced for Franklin Watts by
White-Thomson Publishing Ltd
210 High Street
Lewes BN7 2NH

Editor: Rachel Minay
Designed by: Tinstar Design Ltd
Picture research: Morgan Interactive Ltd
Consultant: Frank Blackburn
Printed in: China

**British Library Cataloguing
in Publication Data**
A CIP catalogue record for this book is
available from the British Library.

ISBN: 0 7496 6064 3

Acknowledgements
The publishers would like to thank
the following for permission to
reproduce these photographs:

Ecoscene
FC, 1 (Laura Sivell), 4–5 (Robert Pickett),
6 (Peter Bond), 7 (Lando Pescatori), 8, 9,
10 (Robert Pickett), 11 (Robin Williams),
12 (Robert Pickett), 13 (Dennis Johnstone),
14 (John Farmar), 15 (Laura Sivell),
16 (Alastair Shay), 17 (Jamie Harron),
18 (Robert Pickett), 20 (Laura Sivell),
21 (Anthony Cooper), 22 (Chinch
Gryniewicz), 23 (Andrew Brown),
24 (Rosemary Greenwood), 25,
27 (Robert Pickett), 28 (Laura Sivell),
29 (Frank Blackburn);

Nature Picture Library
19 (Paul Hobson), 26 (Mark Payne Gill).

Every effort has been made to contact copyright
holders of any material reproduced in this book.
Any omissions will be rectified in subsequent
printings if notice is given to the publishers.

Contents

Butterflies

Butterflies are among the most colourful visitors to gardens in the summer. They flutter from flower to flower in search of food. They are found all over Britain and live in the countryside as well as in towns and cities.

Butterflies are insects

The butterfly is an insect. Insects are invertebrates, animals without backbones. The body of an insect is made up of three parts – the head, thorax and abdomen (see opposite page), with three pairs of legs. Most insects have two pairs of wings attached to their thorax.

antenna or feeler

leg

proboscis

The Brimstone butterfly has large yellow wings.

4

wing

ANIMAL **FACTS**

▶ *In Britain there are 56 native species or types of butterfly. Also there are three species that are regular visitors, flying over the English Channel from Europe, and nine species that visit very occasionally.*

Life cycle

The life cycle of the butterfly has four separate stages — egg, caterpillar or larva, pupa and adult. The egg hatches into a caterpillar that looks completely different from an adult butterfly. The caterpillar has to change its body shape to become a butterfly. This is called metamorphosis.

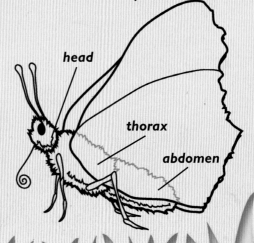

head

thorax

abdomen

Butterflies are insects

There are millions of different types of insect. They range in size from tiny fleas to huge stag beetles.

Head, thorax and abdomen

The head of an insect has two compound eyes (see page 22), a pair of antennae and mouthparts for feeding. Mouthparts vary, depending on the insect's diet. Some have strong jaws for chewing grass, for example grasshoppers. Honeybees and houseflies have tube-like mouthparts designed to suck up liquid. An insect's legs and wings are attached to its thorax, which joins the head to the abdomen.

This pair of Silver Studded Blue butterflies are using their long slender legs to clamber over this flower.

ANIMAL **FACTS**

▶ *Britain's largest butterfly is the Swallowtail, which has a wingspan of about 80 mm.*

Wings

Most insects have two pairs of wings. The wings of butterflies and moths are the largest of all the insects. Beetles have a hard pair of outer wings to protect a pair of delicate wings, which lie underneath. Flies only have one pair of wings and some insects don't have any wings at all.

animal **CLUES**

Butterfly or moth?

Most moths fly at night while butterflies are active during the day.

A butterfly's antenna has a broad tip at its end. A moth's antenna does not. Some male moths have feathery antennae.

The ladybird is an insect and uses its delicate pair of wings to fly.

Laying eggs

The first butterflies appear on warm days in spring. The male and female butterflies mate. Then the female butterfly lays her eggs.

The female butterfly lays her eggs on a plant that the caterpillars can eat after they hatch. The eggs of the Small Tortoiseshell, Red Admiral, Peacock and Comma are laid on nettles, while the Large White butterfly lays her eggs on cabbage plants. Some butterflies lay each egg in a different place, but most lay their eggs in groups of between 30 and 200.

The female butterfly chooses where to lay her eggs very carefully.

ANIMAL **FACTS**

▸ *As many as 1,000 eggs may be laid by the Small Tortoiseshell butterfly.*

The eggs of the Large White butterfly turn more yellow as they develop.

Butterflies lay different eggs

Each type of butterfly can be identified by its egg. The eggs of the Small Tortoiseshell butterfly are pale green with eight or nine ridges running from top to bottom. The Clouded Yellow lays pale yellow eggs that turn orange just before they hatch.

animal CLUES

Watch out for butterflies laying their eggs on nettles. The Peacock and Small Tortoiseshell lay their eggs in groups under the leaf while the Comma lays her eggs on the top. The Red Admiral lays a single egg on top of the leaf.

Eggs hatch into caterpillars

After one or two weeks butterfly eggs hatch into caterpillars. The caterpillar is the growing and eating stage in the butterfly's life cycle.

Caterpillars

A caterpillar has a long body made up of sections called segments. There is a head, thorax and abdomen, just like the adult butterfly. It has six legs attached to the thorax. Each leg ends in a claw. Further back there are four pairs of fleshy prolegs. They are attached to the abdomen and each one ends in tiny curved hooks. At the end of the abdomen is a clasper. The prolegs and clasper help the caterpillar to grip as it crawls along branches and leaves.

SCIENCE LINKS

The tiny hooks on the bottom of each proleg work like Velcro. They stick to things and become firmly attached but they can be pulled off easily. This helps the caterpillar to move across slippery surfaces.

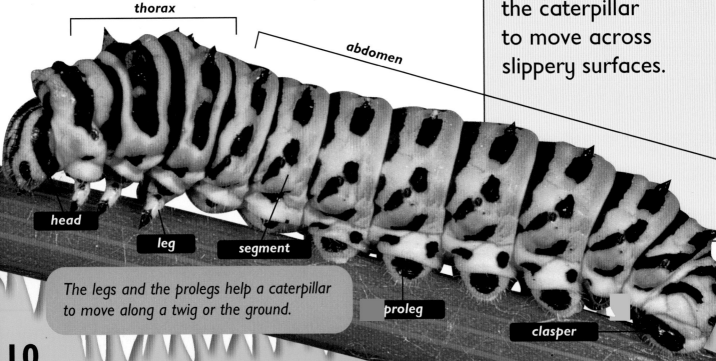

thorax

abdomen

head

leg

segment

proleg

clasper

The legs and the prolegs help a caterpillar to move along a twig or the ground.

Small Tortoiseshell caterpillars stay together and spin a silken tent around a few nettle leaves for protection.

Caterpillar jaws and eyes

Caterpillars start eating as soon as they hatch and they eat all day! Their jaws are strong and sharp to tear through leaves and bark. Caterpillars do not have compound eyes. Instead they have a number of simple eyes on each side of the head, which allow them to detect light and dark.

ANIMAL **FACTS**

▶ **As few as one out of every 100 butterfly eggs may hatch. The rest are eaten by predators (see pages 20–21) or killed by disease.**

Caterpillars, pupae and butterflies

Caterpillars eat a lot of food and grow rapidly. After a month they enter the next stage of the life cycle, the pupa.

The pupal stage

Once the caterpillar is fully grown, it pupates. Most caterpillars pupate while hanging from a branch or leaf. Some others spin a silken cocoon around themselves before they pupate. A few caterpillars pupate on the ground.

ANIMAL **FACTS**

▶ *The skin of a caterpillar is tough and does not expand much. To grow, a caterpillar has to shed or moult its skin about four times before it is fully grown.*

Some caterpillars pupate on a plant. Inside the pupa the caterpillar's body changes.

The pupal stage is a time of change. From the outside it looks as if nothing is happening, but inside the pupa, the body of the caterpillar is being rearranged to form a butterfly.

A new butterfly

After a few weeks, the pupal case splits and a butterfly pulls itself free. It crawls onto a nearby branch. Its wings are crumpled and wet so it cannot fly. The butterfly has to pump blood into its wings so that they expand. Once they are dry the butterfly can fly away.

Here a Swallowtail butterfly has emerged from the pupa and is drying its wings.

science LINKS

Butterflies undergo metamorphosis. They are not the only animals to do this. How many other animals do you know that go through metamorphosis?

Where are they found?

Butterflies are found across Britain in many different types of habitat.

Butterfly habitats

Most butterflies are found living in grassland, farmland and woodland habitats. These are habitats where there are lots of flowers in summer. Some butterflies, for example the Mountain Ringlet and the Scotch Argus, can be found on mountains. These butterflies have adapted to the cold conditions and have learnt to fly in bad weather.

The Small Tortoiseshell is attracted to gardens where it finds plenty of flowers with nectar.

The Scotch Argus is found in the west of Scotland, living on grassy hillsides, sheltered valleys and moors.

Attracting butterflies

Many types of butterfly come into gardens and parks. Butterflies are attracted by flowers that produce lots of nectar and by plants on which they can lay their eggs, for example nettles. Gardeners can attract butterflies into their gardens by growing plants such as the butterfly bush (buddleia), ice plants, Michaelmas daisies, honeysuckle and tobacco plants.

ANIMAL **FACTS**

▶ **A garden can be visited by as many as 20 different species of butterfly in the course of a year.**

Butterfly movement

Butterflies have a tough outer covering called an exoskeleton that protects their body.

Moving

Butterfly muscles are found inside their exoskeleton. These muscles move their wings and legs. Each leg is made up of many small sections connected together at joints. The joints allow the leg to bend. Butterflies use their legs to walk over flowers and leaves in search of food. They have tiny claws at the end of their legs to grip the surface when they land.

A butterfly has two pairs of wings — four wings in total. On each side of the body, the front and back wings are hooked together, so they move as one when they are flapped. It looks like the butterfly has a single pair of wings.

science LINKS

Butterflies move their wings up and down to stay in the air. How do the wings of a plane differ from those of a butterfly?

Two pairs of wings

Butterflies have two pairs of wings, which they use to fly. When a butterfly flaps its wings up and down it is lifted into the air. Most butterflies beat their wings just 10 times every second. This is much slower than many small insects such as flies. Butterflies are good fliers and they can travel long distances. Many cross the English Channel from Europe in summer to breed in Britain.

ANIMAL **FACTS**

▶ *Some butterflies can travel distances of up to 3,000 km.*

The wings are covered in rows of tiny scales, the size of dust. They are arranged like tiles on a roof. The pigment in the scales and the way light reflects off them give the wings their colour.

Finding food

Adult butterflies eat very little during their short lives, which can range from a few hours to several months. They survive on mostly plant nectar, juice from rotting fruits and sap from trees.

Finding nectar

Many flowers produce a sugary liquid called nectar. This is an energy food that butterflies love and they fly from flower to flower in search of it. Butterflies like flowers that are open and large enough for them to land on.

This butterfly is searching from flower to flower to find nectar.

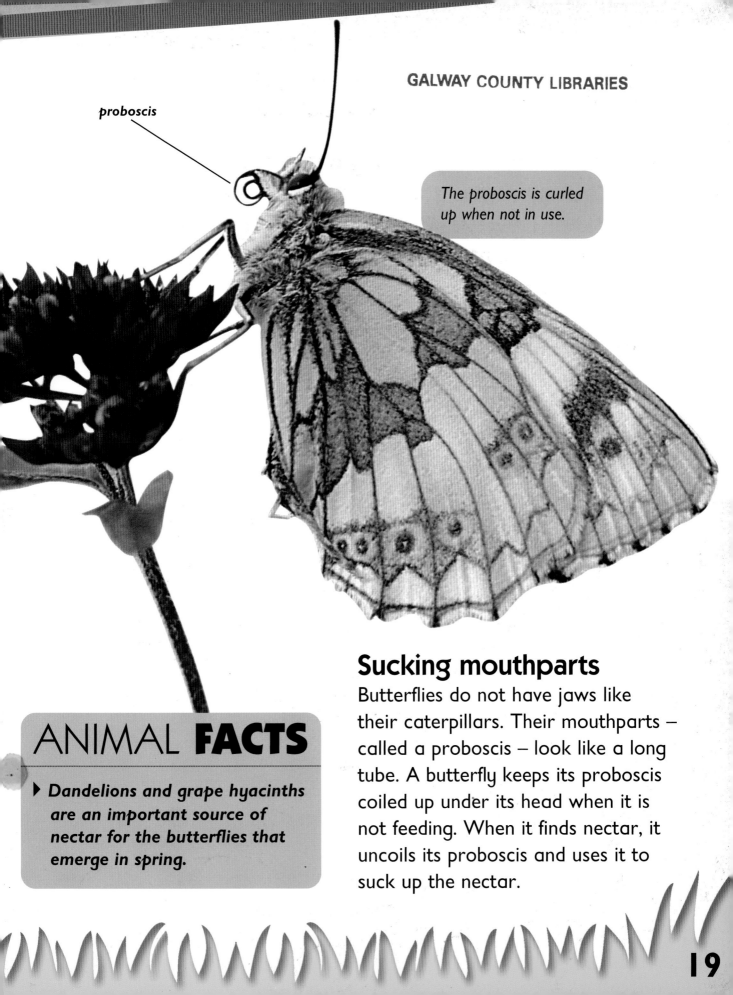

proboscis

The proboscis is curled up when not in use.

Sucking mouthparts

Butterflies do not have jaws like their caterpillars. Their mouthparts – called a proboscis – look like a long tube. A butterfly keeps its proboscis coiled up under its head when it is not feeding. When it finds nectar, it uncoils its proboscis and uses it to suck up the nectar.

ANIMAL **FACTS**

▶ Dandelions and grape hyacinths are an important source of nectar for the butterflies that emerge in spring.

Food chains

Butterflies and caterpillars are important animals in food chains. They are called primary consumers because they feed off plants. Primary consumers are eaten by animals higher up the food chain.

Which animals eat butterflies?

Butterflies and caterpillars have many predators. Birds catch butterflies as they fly from flower to flower. Sometimes butterflies fly into a spider's web and get eaten by the spider. Lizards and snakes eat butterflies too. However, butterflies have small bodies so they are not as nutritious as the plump caterpillars.

Plants are called producers because they make food for animals such as insects.

Many animals eat caterpillars

Caterpillars are an important food for many animals. In summer, animals – especially small birds such as tits and robins – catch caterpillars to feed their young. Without a plentiful supply of caterpillars many animals would starve.

A robin takes a caterpillar to its young in the nest box.

ANIMAL FACTS

▶ *A pair of blue tits feeding their young collect one caterpillar every minute. This means they may collect as many as 10,000 caterpillars while their chicks are in the nest.*

Sensing the world

Butterflies need senses to find their way around and to survive.

Compound eyes

Butterflies have two compound eyes. These are large eyes made up of lots of tiny eyes joined together. Their eyes are good at seeing red, the colour of many flowers. They can also see colours that we cannot, such as ultraviolet. This means that butterflies see flowers very differently to us.

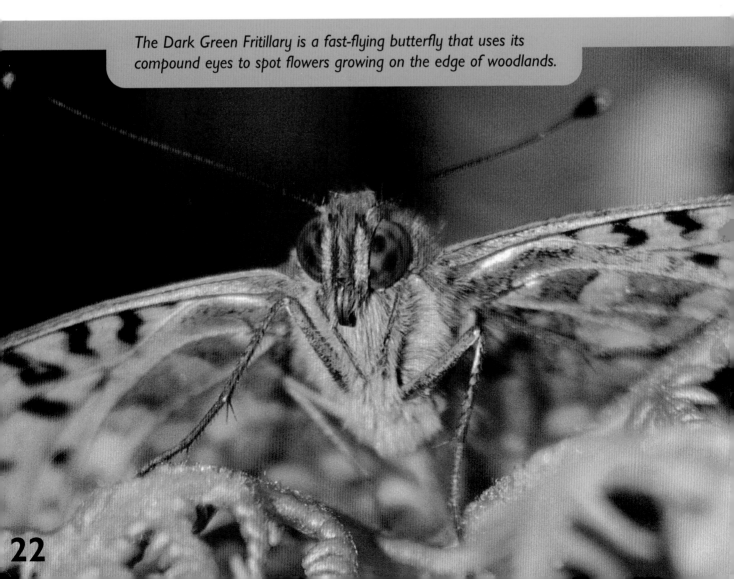

The Dark Green Fritillary is a fast-flying butterfly that uses its compound eyes to spot flowers growing on the edge of woodlands.

Smelling and tasting

Butterflies have a pair of long antennae that they use to detect smells in the air. The butterfly does not have taste buds on its proboscis. Instead its taste buds are found on its feet. When the butterfly lands on something, it tastes it straight away to see if it is a good source of food.

ANIMAL **FACTS**

▶ *A male butterfly can pick up the scent of a female from as far away as 11 km.*

science **LINKS**

Two eyes help us judge distances. Cover up one eye and try to pick up something with your hand. Is it easier or more difficult to do this with one eye closed? Why does the butterfly need to be able to judge distances?

Each butterfly antenna contains 40,000 tiny receptors that are connected to nerves.

Protecting themselves

Butterflies and caterpillars have ways of protecting themselves from predators. Some use poison while others rely on disguise.

Warning colours

The colouring of some butterfly wings is designed to scare away predators. The Peacock butterfly flashes open its wings to reveal two large blue eyespots. This sudden movement can be enough to put off a bird.

The 'false eyes' on the hind wings of the Peacock can scare away birds.

The Comma butterfly has wings with a ragged edge. It looks as if the wings have been torn on brambles but in fact this is the perfect disguise for hiding in the hedgerow.

Camouflaged

Some butterflies and caterpillars are coloured so that they blend into the background and they cannot be spotted by their predators. Green caterpillars are able to hide on leaves while the grey and brown colours of the Grayling butterfly blend perfectly with sandy soil. These caterpillars and butterflies are incredibly difficult to spot if they stay perfectly still.

Poisonous caterpillars

Many caterpillars are poisonous. They get the poison from the plants they eat. Their bright colours are a warning to predators that they are not to be eaten. Some caterpillars are very spiky or hairy and this makes them difficult to eat.

Keeping warm

Butterflies need warm weather. In the morning they warm up their bodies by holding their wings out in the sun. They do not fly on cold days and are only active during the spring and summer months of the year.

Surviving the winter

Winter weather is too cold for butterflies. Most butterflies die in autumn after the first frosts. However their eggs and pupae can survive the winter. Some lie just under the ground in the soil. Their life cycle is completed in spring.

This Red Admiral butterfly has found a sunny patch on a tree trunk.

animal CLUES

Look out for overwintering butterflies in sheds, greenhouses, lofts and under roofs. Don't disturb them!

A few species of butterfly, for example the Small Tortoiseshell, survive the winter by sheltering in sheds, garages and under roofs. In late autumn they find their winter resting place. Once they have settled in place, they do not move and look as if they are dead. These butterflies stay like this all winter and wake up in spring when the weather warms up. Butterflies that overwinter are the first ones to fly in spring.

Butterfly stories

The name 'butterfly' is thought to come from stories dating back to medieval times. In these stories the butterflies were believed to be disguised witches or fairies who stole butter from larders and churns.

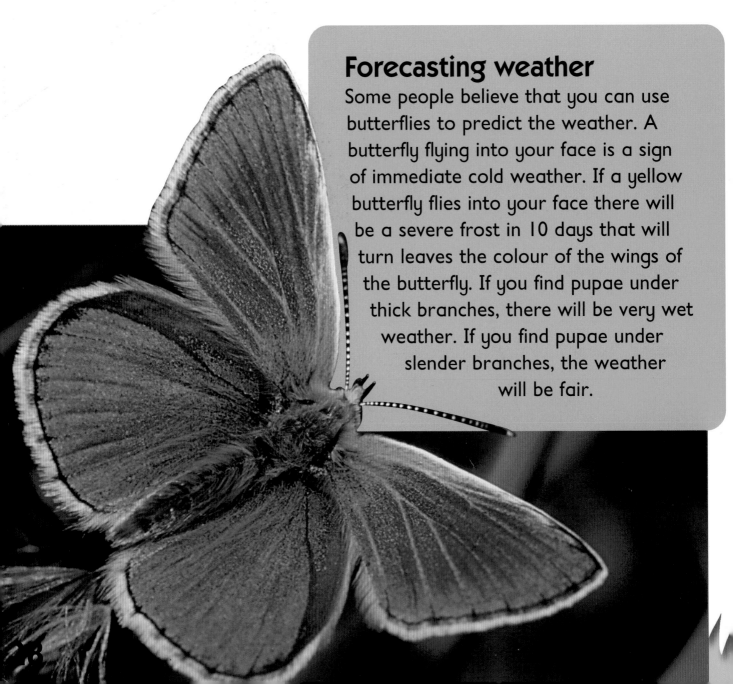

Forecasting weather

Some people believe that you can use butterflies to predict the weather. A butterfly flying into your face is a sign of immediate cold weather. If a yellow butterfly flies into your face there will be a severe frost in 10 days that will turn leaves the colour of the wings of the butterfly. If you find pupae under thick branches, there will be very wet weather. If you find pupae under slender branches, the weather will be fair.

Keeping secrets

There is a Native American story that says: 'If you have a secret wish, capture a butterfly and whisper your wish to it. Since butterflies cannot speak, your secret will always be safe with them. Release the butterfly, and it will carry your wish to the Great Spirit, who alone knows the thoughts of butterflies. By setting the butterfly free, you are helping to restore the balance of nature, and your wish will surely be granted.'

Butterfly facts

Rare or extinct?

Four species of butterfly have become extinct in Britain — the Black Veined White, Large Copper, Mazarine Blue, and Large Tortoiseshell. The Large Blue was extinct in Britain but it was reintroduced in 2000 and is now breeding in nine protected sites. In 2001, Real's Wood White was discovered in Northern Ireland. It was the first time this butterfly had been found in Britain.

BUTTERFLY FEATURES

- *Butterflies are insects.*

- *They have three body parts (head, thorax, abdomen), three pairs of legs and two pairs of wings.*

- *Their life cycle has four stages — egg, caterpillar, pupa and adult.*

- *Butterflies have a proboscis to suck up nectar from flowers.*

- *Butterflies have two compound eyes.*

Butterfly websites

Butterfly Conservation

www.butterfly-conservation.org
The website of Britain's leading butterfly organisation with pages of information on the different types of butterfly, butterfly reserves and conservation.

British Butterflies

www.britishbutterflies.co.uk
A website that shows photos and artwork of all the British species of butterfly.

Note to parents and teachers
Every effort has been made by the Publishers to ensure that these websites are suitable for children; that they are of the highest educational value, and that they contain no inappropriate or offensive material. However, because of the nature of the Internet, it is impossible to guarantee that the contents of these sites will not be altered. We strongly advise that Internet access is supervised by a responsible adult.

Glossary

abdomen the third part of an insect's body, behind the thorax

adapt get used to

antenna (plural antennae) a feeler. Butterflies have two antennae which help them to detect smells

caterpillar the growing stage of a butterfly's life cycle. A caterpillar looks very different from the adult butterfly

clasper the structure at the end of a caterpillar's abdomen – it helps the caterpillar to grip twigs and leaves

food chain feeding relationships between different organisms, for example plants are eaten by caterpillars and caterpillars are eaten by birds

habitat the place where an animal lives

hatch come out of an egg

insect an invertebrate with three body parts and three pairs of legs

mate reproduce

metamorphosis (say: meta-*more*-fuh-*sis*) a change in body shape and appearance, for example when a caterpillar turns into an adult

nectar sweet, sugary liquid produced by flowers

nerve a long thin fibre that carries information to the brain

predator an animal that hunts other animals

prolegs fleshy leg-like structures found on the abdomen of a caterpillar

pupa also called a chrysalis, the stage in a butterfly's life cycle during which the caterpillar changes into an adult butterfly

receptor something that detects changes in the surroundings, for example smells in the air

segment a section (for example, of a body)

thorax the middle body part that joins the head to the abdomen – the legs and wings are attached to the thorax

Index